The
Knockits
of
Knockity Hoo

Maureen Haselhurst
Illustrated by Mark Beech

Chapter 1 – Knockity Hoo

No one had ever seen a Knockit until the day that Jed lost his mobile phone. It happened like this …

Jed and his sister Ava had always wanted to visit the caves at Knockity Hoo. There were strange stories about the place that made it sound very exciting.

"Knockity Hoo," giggled Ava. "What a daft name!"

"It sounds fun," said their Aunt Aggie. "When he gets off the phone we'll talk to Uncle Vince. Let's see if he will take us next weekend."

"Great!" Jed grinned. "Knockity Hoo, here we come!"

Knockity Hoo wasn't easy to find. The caves were tucked away under a hill. The way in was through a dark hole, half hidden in the rocks.

"It looks a bit scary," said Uncle Vince. "Let's see what the information board has to say."

WELCOME TO
KNOCKITY HOO

WELCOME TO KNOCKITY HOO

Old tales tell that these caves are the secret home of Knockits. It is said that these shy, underground folk dug out the caves and that they still live down in the deepest tunnels.

No one has ever seen them but many have heard a strange knocking from deep inside the hill.

"Wow!" gasped Ava. "I wonder if we will we see them. Come on, let's explore!"

The cave was dim and they had to pick their way carefully across the stony floor.

"Whoops!" Jed had tripped. "Oh, no! I've dropped my phone. Where's it gone? I can't see a thing in here!"

Ava flicked her phone open and selected Jed's
number. "This should find it," she said.

It did. A faint ring tone trilled out. It seemed
to be coming from a hole in the floor of the
cave – a hole with steps leading downwards.
It was then that something odd happened.

The phone stopped ringing. Someone had answered it.

"Hello," said a gritty little voice. "This is Digby speaking. Who's that up there?"

They stared at Ava's mobile. Grinning out from the screen was a photo of a cheeky face with wild, spiky hair.

"I don't believe it," squeaked Jed. "It's a Knockit!"

"Who's that up there in the Overground?" asked Digby Knockit again.

"This is Ava speaking." Ava tried to sound cool. "I think you've found my brother's phone. Can you bring it back, please?"

Shan't!

"Shan't! Finders keepers," said the Knockit. "If he wants it, then he must come down here and get it."

"All right!" Jed agreed eagerly.

"You're not going down there by yourself," Aunt Aggie told him. "I'm coming with you."

Jed and his aunt scrambled down the rocky steps. They found themselves in a low tunnel lit by flickering candles. Digby Knockit was nowhere to be seen. He had vanished into the secret nooks of Knockity Hoo.

"Digby!" shouted Jed. "Where are you?" His words echoed off the stony walls.

Someone giggled in the darkness and then came the sound of knocking.

"Can't catch me!" called a voice.

"That's him," said Jed. "Follow that Knockit!"

Where are you?

Can't catch me!

So began a crazy game of Follow-My-Leader as Jed and Aunt Aggie chased after Digby.

"This is the best fun I've had for ages," Jed laughed as they ran through the maze of winding tunnels.

Then the knocking stopped. Digby had done it again. He'd vanished.

"I have no idea where we are," said Aunt Aggie, "but there's a light up ahead. We'll go that way."

"Shh! Listen," said Jed. "I can hear drumming. What's going on?"

They tiptoed along the low tunnel towards the light. Then they turned a sharp corner and came out into a dazzle of sunshine. They were at the bottom of a deep, wide well. Far above their heads, it was open to the summer sky.

The place was packed with dancing Knockits, all knocking out crazy rhythms on the rock walls.

"I think …" shouted Jed above the din, "I think we're at a Knockit party!"

The dancing stopped. The knocking stopped. Everything went quiet as the Knockits stared at Jed and his aunt.

"Grandpa Pit!" one of them yelled. "We've got party-pushers!"

An ancient Knockit came forward. He didn't look at all pleased to see them. This must be Grandpa Pit, thought Jed.

"People from the Overground aren't welcome in the Underground," grunted the old Knockit. "People are noisy and nosy and they dig holes down into our homes."

Aunt Aggie looked cross. "Well," she said, "Jed's a bit noisy and I'm bit nosy. But we never, ever dig holes."

"We're sorry for pushing into your party," added Jed.

"I should jolly well think so!" snapped Grandpa Pit. "You've pushed into our Midsummer Whoopee. This is the only day of the year that the sun shines into Knockity Hoo."

"You could have heaps of parties in the sunshine if you lived in the Overground," Jed pointed out.

Grandpa Pit shook his head. "We're happy with our underground life and with one Whoopee. Now then, off you go!"

He turned back to the Knockits and shouted, "Let's knock!"

"Whoopee!" yelled the Knockits and they began to dance and knock even louder.

"But how can we go?" asked Jed. "We don't know the way out."

"Hello," said a gritty voice. Jed had heard that voice before. Standing next to Jed was …

"Digby!" said Jed in surprise.

The little Knockit grinned. "Here's your people-phone back. It's ace."

At that moment the phone rang.

"Jed, are you all right?" Ava's voice seemed far off. "What's all that noise?"

"We're at a kind of a party."

"Really? Well, if you're at a party, you need music. Hold on …" and the latest dance hit jangled out from Jed's phone.

"Cool!" giggled Digby and he began to knock out a clever beat on the rocks. He was a great drummer.

"People-music is great," he told them. "I wish I could hear more."

Jed smiled at him. "You can, if you show us the way back to the Overground."

Digby's wild, spiky hair stood on end with excitement. He wasn't like other Knockits. He thought that the Overground sounded exciting. He wanted to find out more about it. "All right, I'll do it!" he agreed.

Back along the tunnels and caves of Knockity Hoo they went. Back up the dark, winding stairs and out into the cave where all this had started.

"We've had the best adventure ever," Jed told Ava and Uncle Vince. "The stories about Knockits are true!"

Ava was staring at Digby. "Hi," she said, "I think your hair is really cool."

Digby blushed. He had the feeling that he might get to like people.

Digby began to visit his new friends in the Overground. They played him music and Digby knocked along with the beat.

"You're a great drummer, Digby," Jed told him. "You live in the rocks so you should play in a rock band," he joked.

When Digby went back to the Underground
this time, he had an exciting plan. Soon,
Knockity Hoo was filled with the music of
Digby's very own rock band – *Rock it with
the Knockits.*

"My new rock band is fantastic!" Digby told Jed and Ava the next time he saw them. "Even Grandpa Pit likes us."

Ava laughed. "I'd love to hear you," she said.

Digby blushed. "You can. We're playing at the next Midsummer Whoopee. You can come – if you'd like to."

Would they like to? You bet they would!

The following year, it turned out to be the best ever Midsummer Whoopee. The Underground was filled with the happy sound of really cool music as Jed and Ava partied with the Knockits of Knockity Hoo!